Published by: Boulder Press, P.O. Box 2001, Boulder, CO 80305

Photography and Text © 2008 Mike Barton

Individual prints may be purchased directly from the photographer: mikebartonphoto@yahoo.com or 720 934-4322.
Photographer's website: www.mikebartonphoto.com.

Library of Congress Catalog Card Number: 2007940590
ISBN 13: 978-0-9801024-0-6
ISBN 10: 0-9801024-0-5
First Printing: 2008
Created and designed in the United States.
Printed in Canada.

impressions

BOULDER

foreword by Olympic Gold Medalist Frank Shorter

photography and text by Mike Barton

BOULDER PRESS

Contents

FOREWORD

We residents of Boulder, Colorado truly enjoy showcasing our town. It is a city that invites a visitor's tour because of its natural settings, unique layout and historic locations. It is always fun to take someone from out of town and surprise them with how varied and yet close together so many wonderful places of interest there really are.

I have been active in the Boulder outdoors for 37 years and have covered much of the area on foot and bicycle, so I was curious to see how Mike Barton would view our adopted city through his camera lens. I was truly taken back. With the exception of one scene (I'll let you guess which one), I felt I had been physically at the very spot where the picture was taken.

I enjoy varying my running and bike riding routes and while out there having fun, I have always practiced what psychologists have come to call visualization. To me, it has always been simply using a relaxation technique to think of myself in a competitive situation and let it play out in my mind to a successful outcome. Sometimes months later, in a race when things are going very well, I suddenly sense that I have been in that exact place and situation before and feel much more relaxed and uplifted.

When I read Boulder Impressions, I find myself on a similar visual tour. As I look through the photographs, I find myself thinking "been there, been there" and suddenly feel at home. Now I have a book to carry with me to show people where I actually live and they can see and sense why I am so happy to live here.

Frank Shorter

As a member of the U.S. Olympic marathon team, Frank Shorter won the gold medal at the 1972 Olympic Games and returned to the 1976 Olympics to win the silver medal. After earning his law degree at the University of Florida, he was admitted to the Colorado Bar Association in 1975. Often credited with having spurred the running boom of the 1970s, Shorter now lives in Boulder, Colorado named "America's Best Running City" by Runner's World in January 2001.

BOULDER COLORADO
An Introduction

Tucked against the Rocky Mountain foothills, Boulder has been labeled "the city nestled between the mountains and reality," "the People's Republic of Boulder" and "Little Berkeley." Yet, whatever you call this attractive town, this little city seems to draw people from every direction.

Whether you are an outdoor enthusiast or just want a relaxing getaway, there is something for everyone in Boulder. With more than 43,000 acres of open space land and hundreds of miles of hiking and biking paths traversing around the city, Boulder is an outdoor lover's paradise. You can pursue almost every sport under the sun except surfing. Hikers flock to the vast open space. Others stroll the tree shaded Pearl Street Mall with its quirky shops and world-class restaurants.

With the combination of natural beauty and great year-round weather, Boulder has earned the reputation as a city for the healthy and active lifestyle. It is also known for its unique blend of hippie liberal, yuppie, granola eating, tree hugging, and prairie dog loving attitudes. A place where Dunkin' Donuts goes out of business and oxygen bars thrive.

With all the scenery and everything else going on around Boulder, many people may forget about the university that helped put it all together. That explains all the college kids you see everywhere. The sprawling University of Colorado at Boulder, with its red tiled roofs and Tuscan architecture can be seen from almost everywhere around town. Boulder is first and foremost a college town, providing a constant inflow of young, smart, talented people to the area.

It's not all bad to have 300 days of sunshine per year, 33 more than San Diego. The snow covered trees and foothills that greet you on winter mornings often give way to afternoons warm enough to hike in shorts. Spring is a beautiful time of year where you'll find wildflowers in Chautauqua Meadow and a rainbow of tulips covering the brick walkways along Pearl Street Mall in the heart of Boulder. Summer morning blue skies and mild temperatures are often followed by brief thunderstorms that sneak over the mountains in the afternoon.

If you get tired of Boulder, there are several options within an easy hour or two drive. To the west are several world-class ski resorts including Vail and Breckenridge. Scenic Rocky Mountain National Park makes a great day trip during all seasons. And Denver with all its professional sporting events, nightlife and cultural activities is just over the hill.

After collecting over 5,000 images and about ten parking tickets, I feel that I have captured the best of Boulder. I sincerely hope you enjoy my photos as much as I enjoyed taking them.

RIGHT: Spring is a can't miss time to visit the award winning Pearl Street Mall in historic downtown Boulder.

BELOW: The Bolder Boulder, a Memorial Day classic, attracts over 50,000 racers to the streets of Boulder.

The majestic Boulder Flatirons can be seen from almost every vantage point in town.

ABOVE: North Boulder residents invite deer to graze in a field along Broadway.

RIGHT: The historic Arnett-Fullen House (1877), nicknamed "The Gingerbread House," combines Gothic Revival and Vermicular elements in the design.

Boulder's vast open space makes it ideal for the active lifestyle.

The rough native sandstone towers, sloping, red clay tile roofs give the University of Colorado at Boulder campus an architecture style that can be recognized at a distance.

PEARL STREET MALL

Boulder's Pearl Street Mall is one of the nation's most successful outdoor malls and is a treasured Boulder landmark. The ever-lively four-block mall is the result of a carefully crafted plan to restore the turn-of-the-century historic district, making it the most popular tourist destination in Boulder - a must see for anyone that visits.

If you enjoy quirky shops, art galleries, relaxing in one of the many patio cafes that spill onto the brick walkways, or soaking in the sunshine while watching the passing spectacle, Pearl Street is the place to be.

On warm days and balmy summer evenings, the mall is filled with locals and tourists. Pearl Street is the stage for a number of street entertainers from mimes to musicians and a hangout for Boulder's unusual characters. Performers of all ages play instruments, perform magic and stunts, and sing for the public.

During the spring, Pearl Street Mall is transformed into a tulip garden with what appears to be a carpet of colorful flowers covering the entire four blocks. The summer months offer many special events including concerts, fairs and festivals.

Pearl Street – it's like an amusement park without the rides

Pearl Street – Where friends meet

The pop-jet fountain across from the Boulder Courthouse is fun and refreshing on warm summer days. The pop-jets were added in 2002, the 25th anniversary of Pearl Street Mall.

Bongo the balloon man, a daily fixture in front of the trendy Peppercorn, makes another balloon animal for little Anja with the red hat.

Musicians of all kinds play throughout Pearl Street during summer months. This duo usually plays near the popular Bookend Café that is connected to the Boulder Bookstore.

Children enjoy climbing in the rock garden in front of the Peppercorn store between Broadway and 13th Street.

Pearl Street
expressions

Pearl Street hosts many
special events including
fairs and festivals.

The Boulder Bookstore features more than 100,000 titles, with four floors of books, magazines, cards and gifts. The woodwork, high ceilings, and stained glass windows make for a comfortable and relaxing atmosphere. After shopping, many people head next door to Bookend Café and enjoy a cup of coffee.

Boulder icon "Fast Eddie" Ermoian and his Worlds Famous Chicago Hot Dogs.
The Chicago native turned in his cart and became a downtown goodwill
ambassador in 2007.

A nearly life-sized bronze sculpture of a young woman on a swing by artist George Lundeen is dusted with snow during an early spring snow shower.

One of many street entertainers that perform in front of Boulder Café.

UNIVERSITY OF COLORADO
BOULDER

One of the first things you notice when entering Boulder are the red flagstone buildings on the CU Boulder campus. The campus is often recognized as one of the nation's most beautiful due to its location at the foot of the majestic Boulder Flatirons and distinctive Tuscan architecture.

Oddly enough, the university was third on Boulder's list of enterprises it was seeking to bring economic development. Boulder lost the state capitol to Denver and state penitentiary to Canon City - be careful what you wish for.

The first buildings were designed in Collegiate Gothic style. But with the university quickly expanding and the future architectural style of the campus in question, the university hired architect Charles Klauder in 1919 to develop a master plan. Klauder proposed a unique architectural style that was influenced by the architecture developed in the mountains of northern Italy. The result turned out to be a harmonious fit with the foothills that surround the university. Take an afternoon and stroll the tree-lined walkways that wind through this scenic campus.

The first building on campus, Old Main (1877), once stood all alone on a windswept hill with an unobstructed view of Flatiron Mountains.

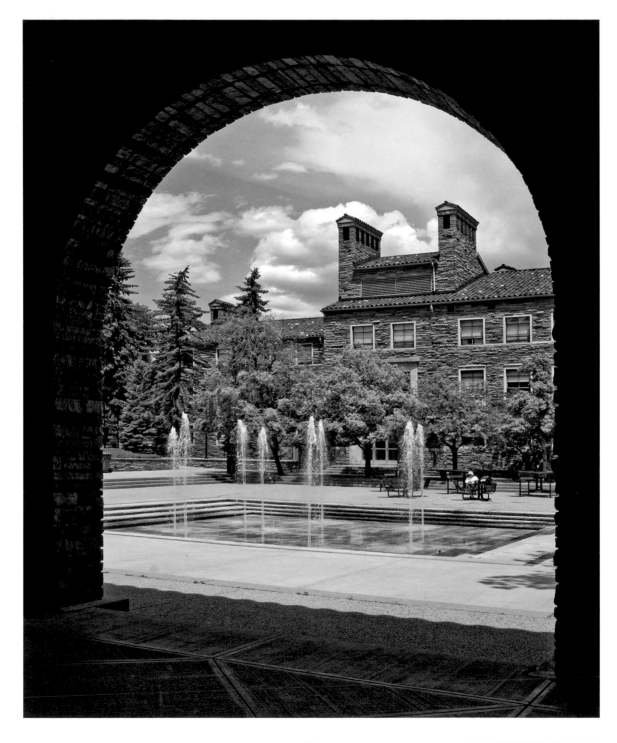

CU students selected the buffalo as the school's mascot in a contest in 1934. Before the buffalo, CU mascots included a goat, mule and bulldog.

Varsity Lake is one of the most scenic settings on campus. In the 1880s, a dam was built across the ravine to give students better access to Old Main. The current arched bridge, made of native sandstone, was built in 1935. It is rumored that a professor brought a canoe from the East Coast after he was fooled by a wide-angle photo taken in 1894, making it look like a huge lake.

ABOVE: CU's 1,300-pound mascot buffalo Ralphie IV runs at full throttle to signal the start of the second half against Big 12 rival Nebraska.

RIGHT: The Hale Science Building (1891) served as a radio-transmission research lab and was built without iron nails to prevent any signal interference.

The historic Macky Auditorium, built in 1914, is one of the premiere concert halls on the Front Range. The design of the auditorium with two large towers is primarily Neo-Gothic, setting itself apart from the rest of the CU campus.

THE HILL

University Hill (The Hill) is the number one hangout for college students. Located just across the street from the university, this part of town would be very different without all the young people who seem to run things around here – it is virtually an extension the CU campus. Even though The Hill is surrounded by one of Boulder's oldest neighborhoods, you might feel a little out of place if you are over 30.

Known as the hub of off-campus social life and for its upbeat nightlife, The Hill has a variety of restaurants, shops, music stores, bars, and coffee houses. Further up The Hill are many fraternities and sororities.

The Hill has a rich history of famous people who worked here when they were students. Robert Redford was a janitor at the Sink restaurant when he came to CU on a baseball scholarship in 1955.

CHAUTAUQUA PARK

Where the present meets the past. Located at the base of the majestic Flatiron Mountains with unparalleled views, tree-lined streets and enchanting turn-of-the-century cottages, Chautauqua Park offers paradise for runners, hikers, rock climbers and photographers.

The Colorado Chautauqua in Boulder was created as a cultural and educational summer retreat in 1898. Today, the Colorado Chautauqua is one of only three remaining Chautauquas in the United States, and the only site west of the Mississippi River in continuous operation. More than 60 of the original cottages and two lodges are still in use today.

Chautauqua Park is also the home of the Chautauqua Summer Festival and the Colorado Music Festival and is a popular gateway to Boulder Open Space trails. The Chautauqua Ranger Cottage, located at the base of the meadow, is a good place to learn more about the area and obtain maps of nearby trails.

One of the many historic cottages built near the turn-of-the century.

After the snow melts in the spring, wildflowers pop up in Chautauqua meadow.

One of Chautauqua's first buildings, the polygon-shaped Auditorium (1898), has long been the site for plays, concerts, movies, lectures and the renowned Chautauqua Summer Festival.

The Dining Hall, built in 1898, is often filled with hungry early-morning hikers.

BOLDER BOULDER

Every Memorial Day, over 50,000 runners, some serious and many silly, take to the streets of Boulder in one of the world's largest road races. While the elite runners compete for the chance to win large prize purses, the vast majority are there to just have some fun. Thousands of costumed crazies join weekend runners and people just out for an early morning stroll.

Everything from Elvis Presley look-a-likes to superheroes to belly dancers will line the course. I heard that someone cartwheeled the whole 10K course and that a little frightened deer was seen running among the friendly crowd.

As the giant wave of fun, athleticism, craziness and determination flows through the streets and neighborhoods of Boulder, they are cheered and encouraged by thousands of spectators along a meandering course dotted with various local bands, cheerleaders and other entertainers.

It all started back in 1979 at the suggestion of Olympic Gold Medalists Frank Shorter. The Bolder Boulder is open to everyone and includes a wheelchair and a walkers' race.

Tens of thousands of spectators watch racers enter Folsom Field and cross the finish line.

BOULDER CREEK

Boulder Creek is a convenient place for residents and visitors to gather and enjoy a variety of outdoor activities. With CU Boulder and Pearl Street Mall located just a few blocks away, the paths and parks along Boulder Creek are usually filled with people of all ages.

The highlight is the 16-mile Boulder Creek Path, a popular place to run, walk and bike, that follows the tree-shaded creek through the heart of the city. The path is mostly flat through the city with several parks and picnic areas nestled along the banks of the creek.

On the west end of town, the path winds up hill for a few miles through Boulder Canyon where many people stop along the way to rest or watch rock climbers scale the canyon walls.

During the spring and summer, many people kayak and tube down the creek, providing hours of entertainment for the spectators that gather along the creek to watch them negotiate many of the small waterfalls along the way.

An angler works the current seams on a beautiful fall morning. Boulder Creek offers a perfect spot to relax and fish without even leaving the city

The icy cold water drops 70 feet into Middle Boulder Creek at Boulders Falls, just 11 miles up the canyon from downtown Boulder.

DUSHANBE TEAHOUSE

Nestled along 13th Street near the heart of downtown Boulder is the beautiful Dushanbe Teahouse. The Teahouse was a gift from Boulder's sister city Dushanbe in Tajikistan while it was still part of the Soviet Union. Over 40 Tajik artisans, with skills handed down from generation to generation, designed and built the teahouse in Dushanbe and shipped it in pieces to Boulder in 1990.

After a long search for the perfect location in Boulder, the teahouse was re-assembled under the supervision of Tajik artists. The Teahouse officially opened in 1998 and is now a full-service restaurant, attracting more than 100,000 visitors each year. It's a stunning, one of a kind place to enjoy a cup of tea - over 100 types of teas are served.

The interior is a dazzling display of vibrant colors with hand-carved painted ceilings and pillars, Persian carpets, art and traditional furniture, including a fountain surrounded by seven copper sculptures. Outside the Teahouse, visitors can wander and enjoy the beautiful rose garden or dine under the shade trees along Boulder Creek.

ABOVE: With colorful ceramic panels, flowers and grapevines, the outside of the Teahouse is as beautiful as the inside.

LEFT: The popular coffee and tea bar, tucked into the back right corner, was handcrafted by the father of Lenny Martinelli, the Teahouse proprietor.

Several cedar columns were shipped 2,000 miles from Lake Baykal to Dushanbe where they were hand-carved before making the trip to Boulder. The colorful hand-carved and hand-painted ceiling is a masterful display of Tajik artistry.

HOTEL BOULDERADO

Boulder's first luxury hotel opened on New Years Day 1909 and has been restored to its original turn-of-the-century condition. As you enter the lobby, your eyes are immediately drawn to the vibrant leaded-glass ceiling, cantilevered cherry staircase and woodwork throughout the main level. Expansions in 1985 and 1989 nearly quadrupled the number of rooms while maintaining the early 20th-century theme.

Located in Boulder's downtown historic district, the hotel is just one block from the award winning Pearl Street Mall where guests can enjoy a variety of restaurants, galleries, patio cafes and places to shop.

The name Hotel Boulderado was formed by combining the city "Boulder" and state "Colorado" so that guests would not forget where they stayed.

HISTORIC NEIGHBORHOODS

Throughout the mid and late 1800s, residential Boulder grew rapidly. Today, many of the beautiful homes built during that era are still around today.

Whittier is one of the oldest neighborhoods in Boulder, with roots dating back to 1859. The neighborhood is known for its large, architect-designed homes and smaller classical-style houses.

Another popular suburb sprang up on Mapleton Hill in 1882. It's hard to believe that this mature tree-lined neighborhood was once an area considered "windswept and barren."

While houses were spreading north of town, University Hill was becoming a fashionable place to live and started to fill in the landscape across from the growing university. A real estate boom in the early 1900's, sparked by the opening of the Colorado Chautauqua and a street car line, led to the construction of many homes on University Hill.

The stately Queen Ann and Victorian homes, canopied by towering maple and cottonwood trees, provides a perfect setting to explore and discover the character of these vintage Boulder neighborhoods.

LEFT: Constructed from local river rock and field stone with 20-inch thick walls, the Squires-Tourtellot House (1865) on Spruce Street is believed to be Boulder's oldest extant home.

BELOW: The eclectic Lewis-Cobb House on Mapleton Hill reflects turn-of-the century style. The hand chipped brick exterior features Flemish bond brickwork.

Named the Castle House due the castellated roofline and octagonal towers, was built by master brick mason Benjamin Gregg.

Built in 1882 with its asymmetrical roofline, wrap-around porch and clapboard shingle exterior, this Victorian house exemplifies the Queen Ann style. The house became famous in the 1970's when it was used for the exterior shots in the TV show Mork and Mindy. It is still one of the most popular tourist stops even though you can't go inside.

CREEK FESTIVALS

One of Boulder's largest and most popular events started as a community creek cleanup day in the mid 1980's with a few hundred people cleaning debris from Boulder Creek. Somehow, the Boulder Creek Festival turned into a Memorial Day weekend event that attracts well over 250,000 people, more than 500 vendors and 70 bands. Now, cleanup day is after the festival.

The Boulder Hometown Fair, held on Labor Day, is a scaled down version of the Boulder Creek Festival. Both events are tucked along Boulder Creek near downtown Boulder. You'll find everything from handmade crafts to fine art to live music. Kids can take part in face painting, amusement park rides and a children's fishing derby.

LEFT: Kids decorate their zucchini cars for the Great Zucchini Race at the Boulder Hometown Fair.

BELOW: Young rock climbers negotiate the climbing wall with the Flatirons in the background.

ABOVE: Visitors browse the tent-covered Art Gallery at the Boulder Creek Festival.

RIGHT: Festival entertainer takes a short break during the three-day long event.

FARMERS MARKET

Surrounded by tall trees near the meandering Boulder Creek, the Farmers Market in Boulder comes alive every Saturday morning during the spring, summer and fall. Hundreds of people make it the place to gather, browse and shop each week. Local farmers bring fruits and vegetables, flowers, plants, wine and cheese.

For many years, the Farmers Market was located near the courthouse on Pearl Street, but with limited parking and competition from Pearl Street Mall, the market had little success. The current location along 13th Street between Canyon and Arapahoe gives the Farmers Market its own identity.

The Farmers Market is always busy on Saturday mornings in Boulder.

BOULDER OPEN SPACE

If you are looking for a hike with a view, Boulder Open Space and Mountain Parks has over 130 miles of scenic hiking trails for all skill levels that traverse the surrounding landscape and meander through beautiful forests. For the cyclist, there are over 200 miles of trails and bike paths with varying levels of difficulty. All trails are well marked for hikers and cyclists alike. Picnicking and fishing areas are also found throughout the parks.

Boulder residents and visitors enjoy over 43,000 acres of open space land thanks to the land preservation programs beginning over 100 years ago.

The Wonderland Lake Trail in north Boulder is popular for running, walking and biking. Many people make the 1.7- mile loop around the scenic lake part of their daily routine, taking in the nice views of Wonderland Lake and the rolling hills along Dakota Ridge. The trail connects to many miles of hiking trails that head into nearby foothills.

Located on Flagstaff Mountain, Sunrise Circle Amphitheater is only a few miles up the hill from downtown Boulder.

There are more of these playful prairie dogs around Boulder than liberals.

Sawhill Ponds are the result of a gravel mining operation and reclamation project. When the mining stopped, groundwater filled the sculpted remains, creating a wetland area that provides habitat for many species of wildlife.

The lush streamside McClintock Trail begins near the historic Chautauqua Auditorium.

Boulder Open Space is friendly to dogs of all sizes. The popular Mount Sanitas loop has spectacular views of Boulder and the Indians Peaks range.

BOULDER RESERVOIR

Boulder Reservoir is where Boulder residents and visitors go for boating, swimming, sunbathing and to enjoy a picnic. One can easily kick back on a beach chair surrounded only by the laughter of children and the distant hum of powerboats in the reservoir. The reservoir is located just north of Boulder.

Every spring, a local radio station hosts the wacky Boulder Kinetics. Teams dressed in crazy costumes race around the reservoir in homemade kinetically designed vehicles. Based on how fast many of them sink, it appears they were never tested on water. One of the awards is called "What Were They Thinking?"

The annual Kinetics Fest held every spring is Boulder's biggest beach party.

Another peaceful winter sunrise on the Boulder Reservoir.

The Boulder Peak Triathlon starts and finishes at the Boulder Reservoir.

ABOVE: The group socializes before the ride at different locations around Boulder and usually end up at a local drinking establishment after the ride.

LEFT: The colorful heavy duty curved framed cruiser bikes come with balloon tires, easy to reach swooping handlebars and seats comfy enough to watch a double feature.

THURSDAY NIGHT CRUISERS

If you see or hear a bunch of crazy cyclists yelling "happy Thursday," ringing bells and honking horns, chances are you have crossed paths with the Thursday Night Cruisers.

The cruiser ride is a social bike ride through downtown and neighborhood streets, bike paths, CU Boulder campus and The Hill. The weekly ride goes all year round with a different theme each week, from hillbilly to Hawaiian. Participation during the summer can approach 500.

Many bikes are customized and decorated, armed with every noisemaker ever invented and outfitted with streamers and baskets. The casual freewheeling spirit of the cruiser group contrasts with the self-seriousness attitude of the typical Boulder cyclist.

NCAR
NATIONAL CENTER FOR ATMOSPHERIC RESEARCH

Woody Allan selected NCAR, designed by architect I.M. Pei, to film part of his futuristic movie "Sleeper." About 20 NCAR staff members were hired to work as silent extras for $20 a day.

The Mesa Lab at NCAR sits on a bluff in southwest Boulder at the foot of the Flatiron Mountains and is visible from everywhere in Boulder. NCAR is dedicated to advance the understanding of weather, climate and Earth systems, from the ocean floor to the Sun's core.

The year-round self-guided audio tours give visitors the opportunity to learn about atmospheric science, the building's architecture and the ecology of the NCAR mesa. There are demonstrations of lightning, tornados and fluid dynamics and a solar eclipse telescope.

Trail Ridge Road, climbing above tree line to an elevation of 12,000 feet, is the highest continually paved highway in the United States. The massive Longs Peak in the background has an elevation of over 14,000 feet and is a popular peak to climb.

BEYOND BOULDER

Boulder's close proximity to several wonderful getaways makes it a convenient place to live and visit. If you like to hike the Continental Divide, climb peaks above 14,000 feet, visit pristine alpine lakes, explore lush canyons, ski in the Rockies or get a close up view of the Rocky Mountains, it's all within an hour's drive from Boulder. You can also visit old mining towns high in the mountains that look almost the same today as they did 100 years ago. Just outside the city limit, farms and scenic lakes dot the countryside.

ROCKY MOUNTAIN NATIONAL PARK

Rocky Mountain National Park features spectacular mountain peaks, alpine valleys, shimmering lakes, a variety of wildlife, wooded forests and mountain tundra with easy access to hiking trails.

The park is located about an hour northwest of Boulder in the Colorado Rockies, just above the charming village of Estes Park. This magnificent showcase of the Rocky Mountains includes the Continental Divide, with elevations above 14,000 feet.

ABOVE: Stanley Hotel in Estes Park

The distant snow-capped peaks above Sprague Lake form part of the Continental Divide.

ABOVE: Dream Lake is a moderate mile and a half snowshoe trek from the Bear Lake parking. Rocky Mountain National Park has several miles of snowshoe trails for all abilities.

RIGHT: Reflections on Dream Lake are rare due to the wind that usually comes down off Hallet Peak and Flattop Mountain. Oddly enough, Flattop Mountain is the jagged peak to the right, not the one on the left with the flat top.

RURAL BOULDER

As the road winds and folds into open meadows, eyes are drawn to the old barns and farms sprinkled around the outskirts of Boulder that once marked a thriving farming community. Every year, rural Boulder seems to back a little further from town. Runners and cyclist have discovered this area as a way to escape the more popular trails near town.

Buffalo graze at a farm north of Boulder. At one time, buffalo roamed throughout the open prairie around Boulder.

Old weathered barns like this are common sights throughout the rural Boulder landscape.

ELDORADO CANYON

If you are in the mood to scale a caynon wall, world-class rock climbing can be found in Eldorado Canyon, just six miles southwest of Boulder. The canyon's natural beauty with miles of trails makes it just as popular for hiking, horseback-riding and biking.

ELDORA SKI RESORT

About a half-hour's ride from downtown Boulder, Eldora offers downhill skiing for all ability levels, a terrain park for snowboarders, a groomed cross-country trail system and skate-ski track.

Eldora is a blast from the past, featuring convenient parking, no lift lines, an old fashion lodge with chair lifts within throwing distance.

INDIAN PEAKS

The Indian Peaks are the saw-tooth snow covered mountain peaks you see from almost everywhere along the Front Range.

Indian Peaks Wilderness, located about 20 miles west of Boulder, is one of the most popular wilderness areas in the country, due to it's close proximity to the Boulder/Denver metro area. It's a convenient place for locals and visitors to snowshoe, hike, backpack and camp in the vast and rugged wilderness.

Sunrise on frozen Red Rock Lake.

MOUNTAIN TOWNS

Boulder was founded in 1868 as a supply town for the mining communities like Nederland and Gold Hill. Buildings with high false fronts and log homes are all part of their rustic charm. Just strolling through these old towns is a throw back to the past. Located about 15 miles up Boulder Canyon is the small town of Nederland. A Dutch mining company that owned several mines in the area named the mining supply town Nederlands. The word Nederland means low lands and at the time, miners had to travel down to the town when they needed more supplies.

Today it is better known as a gateway to outdoor recreation, with some of the best hiking, biking, running and cross country ski trails in Boulder County.

Gold Hill was the site of the first major discovery of gold during the 1859 Colorado Gold Rush. The Gold Hill Store, listed on the National Register of Historic Places, has continuously operated since 1880.

About the Photographer

Mike Barton is a landscape photographer from Boulder, Colorado. Born and raised in Michigan, Mike earned an engineering degree from Michigan State and immediately headed west and settled in California.

While Mike has been capturing landscape images since 1981, he is relatively new to the Colorado photography scene after moving to Boulder in 1998. Mike has accumulated many photographic credits, including covers, and has sold over 1,000 prints. His photography is selling at several locations in Colorado and over the Internet.

Mike's style has been characterized by the vibrant contrasting colors that evoke a sense of energy and joy. It is not unusual to find Mike out shooting well before the sunrise and out past dark, often waiting hours for the ideal conditions or moments.

Mike has taught several photography related workshops but considers himself a lifelong student, learning through experience and experimentation. So he always says – "my best photo is the next one I take."

Acknowledgements

We are happy to thank all of the behind-the-scenes people and businesses who kindly shared their time, support and encouragement.

Chris Williams and Lisa Martinez

Cindy and Harvey Jacobson

Bob and Francine Myers

Douglas Frank

Ina Robbins

Bill and Jeni Trine

Deb Farmer

Ginny Corsi

Connie Wilson

Marsha Badger - RE/MAX Alliance
Broker Associate

Heidi Beasecker

Jody Sarbaugh

Greg, Suzanne, Sam and Joe Barton

The Benardi Group

The Hotel Boulderado

Priscilla McCutcheon

Steve Booth

Peter Wayne

Susan and Jim Avery

Rob Schubert

Gary Grizzard